BRITAIN IN OLD PHOTOGRAPHS

OXFORDSHIRE AT SCHOOL

MALCOLM GRAHAM

SUTTON PUBLISHING LIMITED

OXFORDSHIRE BOOKS

Sutton Publishing Limited
Phoenix Mill · Far Thrupp · Stroud
Gloucestershire · GL5 2BU

XFORDSHIRE BOOKS

First published 1996

Copyright © Malcolm Graham, 1996

Cover photographs:
front: Uffington School boys cultivate their
plots *c.* 1910; *back:* Summertown's
Infants' School girls, December 1924.

British Library Cataloguing in Publication Data
A catalogue record for this book is available from the
British Library.

ISBN 0-7509-1268-5

Typeset in 10/12 Perpetua.
Typesetting and origination by
Sutton Publishing Limited.
Printed in Great Britain by
Ebenezer Baylis, Worcester.

CONTENTS

Children pose for the camera in front of Woodcote Council School in February 1905. Erected in 1899, the building has large windows to provide light and fresh air, reflecting the growing importance of 'hygienic' considerations in the design of schools at the turn of the century.

INTRODUCTION

Although some of Oxfordshire's oldest schools date back to medieval times, few children had the experience of regular education before the nineteenth century. In 1379, William of Wykeham, the founder of New College, incorporated a school for sixteen choristers which, as New College School, is now a flourishing preparatory school. A grammar school was founded with the almshouses at Ewelme in 1437 and, remarkably, survives today as a county primary school, still housed in the original brick building. Charity and grammar schools were eventually to be found in many Oxfordshire communities and, during the eighteenth century, small private schools and Sunday schools added to the number of educational establishments. In 1802, however, 86 out of 187 Oxfordshire parishes (46 per cent) were still without a school of any kind and the schools which did exist served only a tiny proportion of the child population.

Some influential people saw no good reason to extend access to elementary education and as late as 1857 the Bishop of Oxford, Samuel Wilberforce, worried that if everyone became learned and unsuited for the plough, 'the rest of us would have nothing to eat'. Others recognised a duty to build 'a steady, honest, God-fearing, Church-going population' and this mission helped to inspire two voluntary organisations, the British and Foreign Schools Society, founded in 1808, and the National Society for Promoting the Education of the Poor in the Principles of the Established Church (founded 1811). The British Schools were unsectarian, but the schools founded by the National Society insisted on denominational teaching; following the Anglican lead, some Roman Catholic and Wesleyan Schools were also established. By 1833, very few Oxfordshire parishes were without schools, but children's attendance continued to be irregular and, in many places, there was insufficient accommodation. Forster's Education Act in 1870 sought to fill the gaps left by the voluntary system, aiming to provide every child with a school place and requiring the election of rate-supported School Boards in areas where voluntary schools were unable to meet this need. This Act, and subsequent legislation enforcing school attendance, inspired a veritable rash of school building by the supporters of religious education, which succeeded in staving off 'Godless' Board schools in most Oxfordshire villages;

even in Oxford, where nearly one in five children were receiving no education at all in 1871, church schools made herculean efforts to cope with a rising school population until the first Board schools became necessary in 1899.

Educational change in the nineteenth century created a social hierarchy of schools which is still evident a hundred years later in the age of parental choice. Voluntary schools catered mainly for the children of poorer people but, in areas with a higher proportion of artisans and craftsmen, they tended to become more exclusive by charging higher fees or by continuing to charge fees after other schools became free in 1891. Private schools were founded for quite specific social groups and, in Victorian East Oxford, for example, so-called middle-class schools provided for the children of tradespeople; when, however, Warden Simeon was offered a Cowley Road site for the infant public school, St Edward's School, in 1872, he found the situation wholly unsuitable for the superior market that he envisaged. The school moved instead to socially acceptable North Oxford which also attracted the preparatory schools, Summer Fields and the Dragon School, Oxford High School for Girls and the girls' boarding school, Wychwood School.

The elementary school curriculum was dominated by reading, writing and arithmetic, particularly after the Revised Code of 1862 insisted that all government grants, except for school buildings, should be dependent upon attendance and the results of an annual examination by Her Majesty's Inspector based on the Three Rs. Matthew Arnold, the famous poet and an HMI, denounced 'Payment by Results' as fostering teaching by rote, but the system was relaxed only gradually and was not swept away until 1890. Teachers subsequently had a much greater freedom and, by 1898, boys from St Barnabas' School in Oxford were regularly using the local environment in their studies; such innovation was rare, however, and in the late 1940s, the County's Assistant Education Officer, Edith Moorhouse, found that she needed to encourage village schoolteachers to make use of the locality in geography, history and nature study.

Investment in schools in the nineteenth century led inevitably to a growing demand for teachers. A diocesan teacher training college for men was established at Summertown in 1840 and moved to Culham in 1853; its early records indicate the poor status of teaching at the time, with one recruit in 1842 apparently motivated only by the desire to escape from the temptation of drink in his former trade as a cooper. The college worked hard to check students' 'unfortunate brogues' or 'provincial voices' and to turn rude and boyish recruits into submissive and studious trainees. Many other teachers learned on the job as pupil teachers, serving as apprentices to the head teacher for five years from the age of thirteen and perhaps going on to a teacher training college to become fully qualified. In the best circumstances, teaching achieved true professional status by the turn of the century and, at St Barnabas' Boys' School in Oxford for example, staff were preparing reports for parental guidance and having 'conferences' to discuss possible improvements. In remote single teacher schools, however, staff continued to be intellectually and professionally isolated, and this problem was not effectively addressed until after the Second World War.

Apart from the few elementary schoolchildren who won scholarships to grammar schools, secondary education was denied to the pupils of voluntary and Board schools and School Boards were only able to spend rates on elementary schooling. The Education Act of 1902 swept away the School Boards and designated County and County Borough Councils as Local Education Authorities (LEAs) with powers to establish and maintain secondary schools. By the mid-1930s, Oxfordshire County Council had built three completely new secondary schools and major projects in Oxford City included the building of Southfield School for Boys in 1935 and new premises for Milham Ford Girls' School in 1939. The pace of change speeded up after the 1944 Education Act, which gave all eleven year olds the right to secondary education. Oxfordshire offered to experiment with comprehensive education to create viable secondary schools in the county's major towns, but the Government insisted on a tripartite system of grammar, secondary modern and technical schools which Oxford City also adopted. According to the Norwood Report of 1942, the grammar school was best for a child 'interested in learning for its own sake'; the modern school was for the pupil 'who deals more easily with concrete things than with ideas'; and the technical school for the person 'who often has an uncanny insight into the intricacies of mechanism'.

Entrance to grammar school was by selection at 11 plus, and it was perhaps natural for the unselected to be seen or to see themselves as 'failures'; in 1961, Oxford City urged parents to help 'by trying not to be over-anxious for their children to qualify for a particular type of school, or at least by doing everything possible to avoid communicating their anxiety to their children'. Secondary moderns were rarely able to achieve 'parity of esteem' with older established and more generously funded grammar schools, and public opinion gradually turned against selection. Oxfordshire had made grammar schools at Burford and Chipping Norton 'all but fully comprehensive' in 1953 and 1957 respectively and reacted positively when the Labour government asked LEAs to submit plans for comprehensive reorganisation in 1965. The County opted for a two-tier system while Oxford chose a three-tier system with lower, middle and upper schools. These changes involved major upheavals including, for example, the merger of four Banbury secondary schools in 1967 to form Banbury School. Voices continued to be heard denouncing comprehensives, but Oxfordshire County Council as the sole LEA for new Oxfordshire in 1974, respected the decisions made in the 1960s.

Resource problems seem always to have been part of life in schools. At Baulking Board School in 1889, the infants were having to write on broken pieces of slate; eight years later, Her Majesty's Inspector reported solemnly that 'The table used by the

Teacher ought to be provided with a fourth leg'. On 25 January 1909, the head teacher of Kingston Bagpuize School noted in the log book that the temperature in the classroom was 35 degrees Fahrenheit. At many Oxfordshire village schools until the 1950s, water had to be fetched from a pump and staff had no separate toilets. Many of the photographs in this book are therefore a tribute to the work of countless teachers who, often against the odds, have succeeded in preparing their pupils for life beyond the classroom.

The traditional way into and out of the prefect's study at Radley College in the 1950s.

THE LEARNING PROCESS

The teacher addresses her class at Stratton Audley School in February 1905. Teaching, particularly in a small village school, could be a lonely experience with little support at work and few social pleasures outside it; some heads recorded this sense of isolation in their log books and it is evident here in a rather comfortless classroom. Being close to the tortoise stove in winter was a small consolation for the teacher in this case.

A clergyman in the back row. Local vicars came regularly to church schools to give religious instruction, but this visitor to Tackley School in June 1905 may have been a Diocesan Inspector on his rounds.

Waiting in the gallery at East Adderbury School, January 1906. Stepped galleries were a popular feature of mid-nineteenth-century schools, providing suitable facilities for class teaching and object lessons in large schoolrooms.

Gallery lesson at Bix School in May 1905, given by a teacher who obviously moved about too much while the picture was being taken. Wall pictures of a horse and a cow had probably been used in many similar object lessons.

The girls of East Adderbury School sit up straight with hands behind their backs, January 1906. Teaching several classes in a large schoolroom could be very distracting; the solution adopted here was to have adjoining classes facing the opposite way.

Blackboard work at Piddington School, March 1906. Other teaching aids in this crowded schoolroom include the covered grand piano in the foreground and a profusion of charts and pictures on the walls.

Standing in their places at Waterstock School, March 1906; segregation of boys and girls in a small schoolroom.

Learning in the shade on a hot summer's day at Idbury and Fifield School, July 1906.

Outdoor lesson for the children of Churchill and Sarsden School, July 1906.

Lesson in progress at Waterperry School in May 1907. Curtains, drawn back on this occasion, were a simple way of creating separate classrooms, but by no means soundproof. A few visual aids and two struggling houseplants have introduced a little colour into this drab environment.

A temporary distraction at Horspath School in July 1907 as the teacher standing at his desk allows the children to pose for the photographer.

Brize Norton School, July 1912. The wood and glass partition seen here was a common method of dividing large schoolrooms, reducing noise levels and distraction but still giving the head visual oversight of the work going on in other classrooms.

Individual desks in Form IV at Oxford Wesleyan Higher Grade School in 1928, the school's final year. The teacher at the back of the room is Mr A. Waterhouse.

Formal classroom layout at Oxford Central Girls' School in New Inn Hall Street, *c.* 1930.

Circling the globe during a geography lesson at the Headington School for Girls, 1956.

Puzzling out the problem during a lesson at Oxford High School for Girls, July 1957.

A new approach to learning; an open-plan classroom at the award-winning Finmere School opened in 1959.

Role-play at Finmere in November 1959, as one pupil dressed as a shopkeeper estimates the cost of her classmate's shopping.

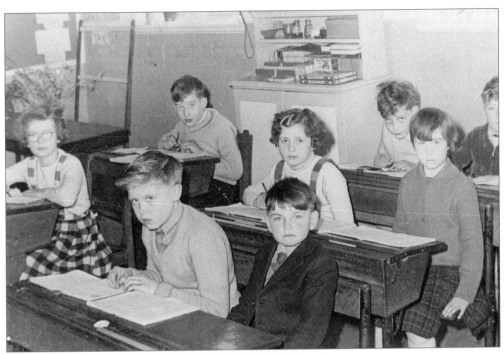

Suspicious looks from the children of Brightwell Baldwin School, February 1961.

Overcrowding in the inadequate classroom of Freeland School, December 1962.

Reading time at Bicester United States Air Force school, 1971.

Children at work and the rocking horse riderless in Eynsham primary school, 1972.

Four girls work up their experiments in the science lab at Oxford High School for Girls, *c.* 1900. Recalling science lessons in this small room, Dorothy Counsell described how 'Miss McDonald was always humorous in her teaching, and we were allowed to talk quietly to one another when weighing and measuring; a most unusual concession in those days'.

The science room at Thame Girls' Grammar School, *c.* 1920.

Chemistry lesson at Banbury County School, 1930s.

Miss Turner and her students in the science laboratory at Oxford High School for Girls, 1948.

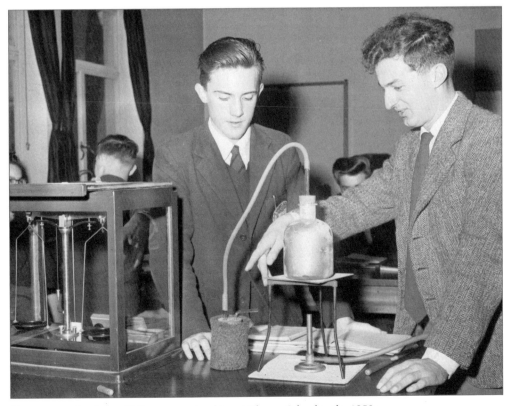

'Do you see what I mean?' One-to-one teaching at Cheney School in the 1950s.

Taking notes in the lab at St Edward's School, 1954.

Outdoor biology lesson at Burford School given by the Head of Science, H.B. Douglas, 1964.

Woodwork under the gas jets at Lord Williams' Grammar School, Thame, 1900s.

Shed-building boys on top of their work at Thame Church of England School, 1920s.

Advanced woodworking lessons at Banbury County School, 1930s.

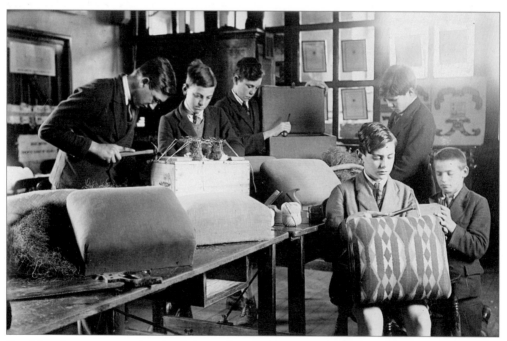

Careful work on seat covers during upholstery classes at Brize Norton School, *c.* 1930.

Children and their teacher in the productive garden of Sibford Gower School in July 1906. A few elementary schools cultivated gardens before the Revised Code of 1862 concentrated teachers' minds on a narrower curriculum. With greater flexibility by the turn of the century, gardening was again encouraged and 79 Oxfordshire schools had gardens by 1910; a shield was awarded each year to the school with the best garden.

Uffington School boys cultivate their plots, *c.* 1910, with the help of BCC (Berkshire County Council) wheelbarrows.

Rest from their labours; boys in the gardening class at Dorchester School take a well-earned breather, 1929.

Bird's eye view of Brize Norton School garden, *c.* 1930, showing the lawn and fruit trees as well as the extensive vegetable plots.

Cooks hard at work in the kitchen of the newly built Sonning Common School, July 1913.

Ready to start; the cookery class with all its utensils at Cropredy School, *c*. 1930.

'Please, miss!' Every hand shoots up during a domestic science class at Hook Norton School, 1936.

All mod cons and school aprons in the kitchen of Headington Council Secondary School, May 1939.

Cooking and ironing for the girls of Boxhill Secondary Modern School in Abingdon, late 1940s.

Sampling the results of a cookery lesson at Oxford High School for Girls in 1948. It is hard to know whether the girls' smiles reflect the achievement of scrumptious success or the brave acceptance of a culinary disaster!

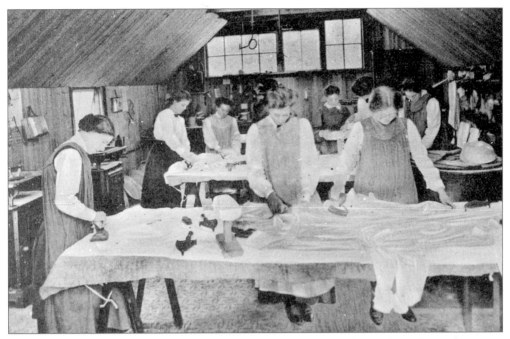

Ironing lessons for the girls of St Katherine's School, Wantage, in the Cookery and Laundry room, 1900s.

Hanging out the washing at Kirtlington School during a laundrywork lesson, 1930s.

Cleaning the bath; instruction in drudgery at the Chipping Norton Domestic Science Centre in 1936.

Hoovering the wall, again at Chipping Norton in 1936, during a practical lesson on the use of the vacuum cleaner.

A lesson in wallpaper pasting and hanging
for a girl from Bicester County School at
the local Domestic Science Centre, 1936.

Washing up in the open air requires enormous concentration at West Oxford School, mid-1950s.

Eyes left for trainee typists at Boxhill Secondary Modern School, late 1940s.

Basket-making at Abingdon Convent School, 1950s. The girl on the right seems to be enjoying an exemption from the task!

Inspection at South Newington School, May 1907. The teacher watches anxiously as the Diocesan Inspector, a local clergyman, questions her pupils and assesses the efficiency of the school.

Closely supervised girls at Oxford High School write purposefully under the watchful eye of Miss Jackson, July 1957.

Success for June Higgins, Head Prefect at Oxford Central Girls' School, at the school prizegiving in the Town Hall in 1947. The Mayoress is giving her the 'C' House Cup for Recitation.

Congratulations to R. Weaver at the City of Oxford School for Boys prizegiving on 30 October 1958. His prize is presented by Sir Bertram Long MC.

ARTS AND MUSIC

Members of the Radley College orchestra and their mascot in 1878. The school's co-founder and first warden, Robert Singleton, encouraged Radley's musical tradition on the grounds that 'the devil hated industry'; he considered that playing instruments was desirable 'provided it did not interfere with cricket and other manly and muscular diversions'.

Art class at Oxford High School for Girls, *c.* 1900.

Morris dancers from East Hanney School, 1900s.

The Pirates of Penzance; the cast of Gilbert and Sullivan's comic opera at the Dragon School in 1914.

Fighting for the boys, nursing for the girls; a display at Clanfield School in 1915 reflecting the impact of the Great War.

Patriotic play staged by children from St Barnabas' School, Oxford, in the grounds of the Radcliffe Infirmary, *c.* 1917. A second performance was given at Garsington Manor, home of Lady Ottoline Morrell.

The cast of *King Rudolpho's Will*, a play performed at the Salesian College in Cowley in July 1920.

Fairies gather in the playground of Summertown Infants' School during the 1920s.

Little Dutch folk created by a change of costume during an international festival at Summertown Infants' School in the 1920s.

Chimney sweeps and a girl sitting cross-legged on the floor contribute to the West Oxford School Carol Concert, December 1929.

The cast of *Aladdin* at Hook Norton School during the summer of 1929.

Marjorie as Puck. She was one of the stars of the Brize Norton School production of *A Midsummer's Night's Dream* in 1930, which had to be repeated by popular demand.

Scandinavian folk dancing at Brize Norton School, 1930.

Brize Norton folk dancers with their trophies in 1930; Mr Jones, the headmaster, is standing on the left.

Statues, busts and stuffed birds; some of the subjects for budding artists in the art room at Banbury County School in the 1930s.

Burford Council School musicians provide the accompaniment for a lone morris dancer in 1935.

The Junior Percussion Band at Burford Council School, 1935.

Christmas play at Churchill and Sarsden School in December 1938, when the cast included a Chinese contingent and a boy with a football as well as angels. The honours board at the back is a reminder of the school's academic aspirations.

Second year pupils at Oxford Central Girls' School dressed up as Red Indians for a performance of *Hiawatha* in 1939.

Maypole dancing in the playground of East Oxford School, 1950s.

Children's fancy dress parade along Church Way, Iffley, 1950s. They are just passing the thatched National School built in 1828.

Scottish dancers in Class II at West Oxford School celebrating the Coronation, June 1953.

House dramatics at Headington School for Girls, 1956.

Don't move; a life drawing class at Headington School for Girls in 1956.

St George on her hobbyhorse sets about the dragon at St Denys School, Oxford, probably during the school's centenary celebrations in July 1957.

Recorder band at St Leonard's School, Banbury, February 1962. The group is accompanied by the headmaster, Mr A.R. Spicer on the piano.

SPORTING LIFE

Jump for it! Radley College only adopted rugby as the main Winter Term sport in 1914 and many of the first XV's early fixtures were against scratch military teams. This line out action took place during a school rugby match between Radley (white shirts) and Eton College in 1918; Radley won easily by 20 points to 6.

Rugger practice for the 1st XV at the Dragon School, Oxford, 1937. The school war memorial and the newly built Dragon barge are visible behind the running three-quarter line.

Scrum down; the scrum half about to put the ball in during a game at the Dragon School in 1957.

Convincing winners of the Oxford Schools football challenge shield in 1913/14, Oxford Wesleyan School beat Cowley 12 nil in the final. The captain, F.H. Dearlove, looks uncomfortable as he tries to hold the shield and keep the ball under control.

Nineteen footballers from St Aldate's School, Oxford, who played for the 1st and 2nd XIs during the 1920/21 season. Their trainer was probably the assistant master, Mr Lewendon.

Protecting his stumps; R.E. 'Chicken' Yates demonstrates the immaculate backward defensive stroke which he perfected while he was at Radley College between 1914 and 1919.

Bat, ball and boaters; well turned-out members of St Edward's School cricket XI in 1875.

A surfeit of bats but no cricket whites for the Clanfield School XI in the 1920s, when Robert Lucas was headmaster (see p. 104) and presumably the team's coach. If the game was played nearby, how often must a cricket ball have ended up in the greenhouse?

Everyone waits for the bowler during a game of cricket at Headington School for Girls in the 1930s.

Aggressive hitting from an Oxford High School girl during a game of playground cricket in 1957.

Bung and hockey game in progress in the playground of Magdalen College School, Oxford, 1881. H.C. Ogle, Master of the school from 1876 to 1896, is the upright figure wearing a mortar board towards the right of the picture.

Hockey players at Magdalen College School, Oxford, 1888. The captain, Tollit (seated centre), has a personalised hockey stick and formidable shin pads.

Awaiting the hit from the touchline; Oxford High School girls playing hockey, *c.* 1900. The high boarded fence around the field ensured that there would be no undesirable spectators.

Netball on the asphalt court; girls at St Katherine's School, Wantage, in position for the play-off, *c.* 1910.

The netball team at Oxford High School for Girls, 1935.

Girls playing rounders at Abingdon Convent School, 1950s.

First service; a doubles match in progress on the playing fields of Thame Girls' Grammar School in the 1900s.

Enjoying tennis at the Dragon School, *c.* 1931. The boy on the left is Leonard Cheshire, the future Group Captain in the RAF, winner of the Victoria Cross and founder of the Cheshire Homes; the other boy is identified only by his surname, Jessel.

The girls of Cheney School's tennis team in the 1950s. Behind the carefully balanced racquets they seem to be reflecting happily upon the season's results.

Gymnasts from the City of Oxford High School for Boys at the Oxford University Gymnasium, *c.* 1900. Headmaster, A.W. Cave, is seated between other members of his staff, E.H. Binney (left) and the Revd H.R. Hall.

Developing their muscles; Oxford High School girls using the apparatus in the school gym, *c.* 1900. The clubs on the far wall were swung in intricate patterns during drill, a daily 10 minute routine which one girl recalled as 'rather dull'.

Parallel bars, ropes and ladders provided for gymnasts at Thame Girls' Grammar School in the 1900s.

Hands above your heads! Physical training class at Hook Norton School in 1929.

Clearing the exercise horse in the gymnasium at Cheney School in the 1950s.

Handstands at a gymnastic display in the grounds of St Denys School, probably at the time of the school's centenary in July 1957.

Legs in the air for Oxford High School girls during physical education, July 1957.

Members of the athletics team from Dorchester School, 1929. They were just off to compete in the county sports meeting at Banbury.

An Olympic Games march past, complete with Nazi-style salute, before the Oxfordshire Schools' Sports Meeting at Chipping Norton in 1932.

The moment of triumph as competitors 443 and 444 are first to the tape at the end of the three-legged race at the Chipping Norton meeting, 1932.

Cup winner, D. Sherlock of Milham Ford
School, with her trophies for hockey and
drill, *c.* 1930.

Sprinting home in the 100 yards race on sports day at the Boxhill Secondary Modern School, Abingdon,
late 1940s.

Radley College VIII at Henley Royal Regatta in 1863. Radley's oarsmen entered the Ladies' Challenge Plate for the first time in 1861 when they were eliminated in the first heat. The 1863 crew was no more successful, losing to Eton College in an event which was eventually won by University College, Oxford.

Magdalen College School IV on the college barge in 1883. From left to right, the people in the back row are
A.F.S. Hunt, T.N. Arkell and W. Kirkby; P. Watson, the cox, and A.F. Titherington are in the front row.

A different foreground to a famous view; Magdalen College School IV with its coach, W.E Sherwood, in
front of Magdalen Tower and Bridge in the mid-1890s.

Members of the St Edward's School VIII cling
uncomfortably to the rungs of a ladder in 1892 as a
novel way of demonstrating their rowing order.

Basil Blackwell, better known for his bookselling business, appears in another guise as coach to the
Magdalen College School IV in 1921. The crew, from left to right, are R.F. Matthews, F.E.W. Toye,
C.J. Highton, C.A. Webb and H.L.W. Middleton.

That sinking feeling; cold, wet and bedraggled Radley College boys escape from their waterlogged boat, *c.* 1922.

Girls learning to swim and practising life-saving in the indoor swimming bath at Thame Girls' Grammar School, *c.* 1920.

River bathing for the boys of Thame Church of England School in the 1920s. In the interests of decency, someone has painted swimming costumes on the boys whose parents could not afford the real thing.

The swimming team from Oxford Wesleyan Higher Grade School with their coach, Harold Spicer, c. 1918. The boys are wearing medals and the captain is proudly holding the shield which Oxford elementary schools competed for each summer.

Swimwear and school uniform modelled by two boys at the Dragon School, *c.* 1930. The number 31 on the swimsuit refers to the boy's hook in the bathing huts beside the river Cherwell, which were to give way to the Dragon Barge in 1936.

A flying header during a diving competition at the Dragon School in the late 1930s. The school had its own bathing place on the Cherwell, and spectators could watch from the river bank or from the barge.

The water polo team from the City of Oxford High School for Boys in 1935/36. From left to right, the back row includes J.F. MacPherson, D. Bleackley, P.J. Lewis, P.G. MacPherson and D.G. Remington; the front row swimmers, also from left to right, are S.J.H. Smith, S.C. Walthew (captain) and I.L. Wheal. Looking overdressed among the swimsuits are the headmaster, J.E. Badham (left), and V.F. Searson, the team's trainer.

Girls from Wychwood School enjoy the use of their bathing place on the Cherwell during the summer of 1947.

Taking the plunge; a student from Cheney School dives into Temple Cowley Baths in the 1950s.

Nail-biting concentration during chess matches at the Boxhill Secondary Modern School at Abingdon in the late 1940s.

Boxing bout in a makeshift ring, again at Boxhill in the 1940s.

An archer from St Denys School, Oxford, aims for the bull during a competition at Bisham Abbey in the 1950s.

Impromptu ice hockey at the Dragon School during a cold spell in 1955.

On guard! Girls from Milham Ford School are taught fencing at Magdalen College School in 1963 by Robert Holmes, Magdalen's Head of PE. This was a pilot scheme for the Duke of Edinburgh's Award.

SCHOOLDAYS

Pupils arriving for another day at Deddington School in June 1904. One little boy, braver or more inquisitive than the rest, has come over to stare in wonder at the photographer, Percy Elford, Oxfordshire's Education Secretary from 1903.

Children queueing for the separate entrances to the boys' and girls' classrooms at Enstone Council School in 1904.

Pupils line up in the playground at Wheatley School before marching into school, June 1905.

The 'Cornwell Conveyance', July 1906; this vehicle was needed to take local children to and from the nearest school in Churchill after Cornwell School closed in 1904.

Bicycles on the rates in 1922! The boys and girls of Bucknell School show off the bikes which Oxfordshire County Council provided for their school journeys.

Passengers for the school bus at Dorchester School, 1929.

Jones of Carterton's bus, which was used in 1929 to transport girls from Brize Norton School to their nearest Cookery Centre.

Lollipop patrol in Burford, as a senior boy sees younger children from the Council School across the High Street, December 1935.

Crossing St Aldate's, Oxford, in the early 1950s; a daily hazard for staff and students when the Oxford Secondary Technical School was based in Church Street, St Ebbe's.

Cyclist meets pedestrians at the beginning of the school day at Cheney School, 1950s.

The act of corporate worship; hymn singing to start the day at Cheney School in the 1950s.

Mid-morning milk break for the girls of
Oxford High School in July 1957.

Do you want peas? Staff at Oxford High School for Girls cope with the queue for dinner in 1957.

Waiting for grace to be said before a meal in Radley College dining hall, 1950s.

Happy faces beneath the oil lamp during school dinner at Chinnor School, 1937.

Dinner forgotten for a moment at Gosford Hill School, Kidlington, 1930s.

Rice and jam; a favourite school pudding which Oxford High School staff seem to be relishing in July 1957.

Austerity Christmas at an Oxford school, which is enjoying food from Tasmania and a visit from the Mayor in the late 1940s.

A West Oxford School teacher and a hopeful pupil accept the welcome gift of a Christmas cake from Australia in December 1952.

Dinner in the village hall for the staff and pupils of Freeland School, which was still without a canteen in December 1962.

Girls and boys come out to play in the playground at Chalgrove School, April 1911.

A rocking horse, scooters and a little truck for the boys of Summertown Infants' School, December 1924.

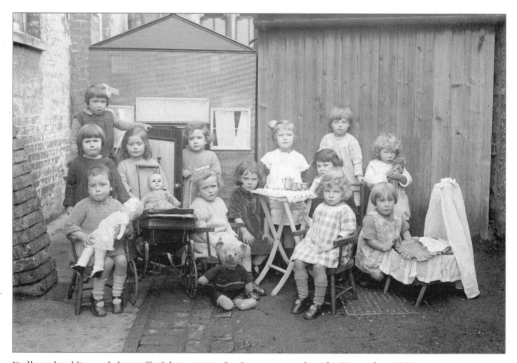

Dolls and teddies and the stuff of domesticity for Summertown's girls, December 1924.

Free activity time for the infants in West Oxford School playground, mid-1950s.

Ring-a-roses and a conspiratorial huddle at Standlake School in 1971.

Creatures from outer space in Ramsden School playground in 1975; the glum faces of most of the children reflect the fact that the school had been judged too small to be viable and was about to close.

Off for the day from Church Hanborough School, 1900.

Camera Club group from St Edward's School on the steps of Water Eaton Manor, June 1904.

A happy group on board the RMS *Majestic* in Southampton Harbour, during a Geographical Society outing from Oxford Central Boys' School in May 1926.

Mr Stevens, a coal merchant at Oxford's Rewley Road station, talks to pupils of Oxford Central Boys' School about the marketing of coal in June 1934; next day, they visited Coventry colliery.

Tour of Croydon Airport in March 1933 for boys from the City of Oxford High School, led by their geography master Mr V.F. Searson.

Pupils from Oxford Central Girls' School at the entrance to Cheddar Gorge, July 1948.

The disused railway station; children from the local school visit the remains of Brize Norton and Bampton station, *c.* 1970.

Katherine Jones and Ian Griffiths from Brize
Norton School meet a one-week-old piglet at
Burford School farm in February 1970.

Map reading problems for students attending
a course at Kilvrough Manor, an Oxfordshire
County Council residential centre on the
Gower Peninsula, *c.* 1970.

Wooden benches rather than easy chairs in Bloxham School's Reading Room, *c.* 1910.

Libraries can be fun; smiles for the photographer in the crowded library of Oxford High School for Girls in 1948.

Rest hour for the girls of Headington School, 1956.

And so to bed; one of the sisters at Abingdon Convent School supervises the boys' bedtime in the 1950s.

TEACHERS AND PUPILS

The teaching staff at Oxford High School for Girls in 1887/88. Miss Soulsby, head of the school from 1887 to 1897, is seated in the centre of the group with Miss Welch to her right and Miss Barratt to her left. On the ground, from left to right, are Miss Mallam, Miss Powell and possibly Miss Johnson.

Mr Liddell (seated centre) and the staff of Oxford Wesleyan Boys' School in the early 1890s. Mr Wake, directly behind the headmaster, went on to become School Attendance Officer for Oxford City.

The headmaster of Bampton Aston School stands contentedly outside his greenhouse in the school garden, July 1905.

Teachers at their desks in Chadlington School, July 1906.

Watlington School staff, June 1911.

Mr Messenger, the bearded headmaster of Little Milton School, meets his counterpart at Great Haseley, Mr Bower, in May 1907.

Mr Lucas and his staff at Clanfield School, 1919. The women teachers, from left to right, are Miss Tibbetts, Doris Hine, Alice Kinchin and Mary Fermor.

Teachers at Dorchester School, 1929.

The gowned headmaster of Banbury County School greets official visitors to the school in the 1930s.

Miss Elliot, a games teacher at Milham Ford School, Oxford, *c*. 1930.

Three generations of headmaster at Brize Norton School, photographed in 1931. From left to right, they are Mr Jones (head, 1925–32), Mr Hawkins (1876–96) and Mr Williams (1896–1925).

Catering staff at Boxhill Secondary Modern School in Abingdon in the late 1940s.

Time for a cuppa in the staffroom at Oxford High School for Girls, July 1957.

Standard II at Lewknor, *c.* 1880. The only identified figure is Elizabeth Ravenning who is seated second from right in the second row. The teacher standing on the right is perhaps the school's assistant mistress, Ada Gulliver, and the head, William Galbraith, may be the man peering through the back row.

Summertown Girls' School, 1876. A compact huddle of pupils with teacher, Rosa Ingle, who was head of the school from 1861 to 1905.

The blackboard helps to locate and date this photograph as being Combe School in 1880; the burly figure on the right is the boys' teacher, Mr Hughes.

An early Dragon School group in 1882, when the North Oxford preparatory school was still called The Oxford Little Boys' School. A committee of Oxford dons founded the school in 1877 and the Revd A.E. Clarke (seated centre) was the first headmaster.

Sailor suits a speciality in Miss Mallam's kindergarten class at Oxford High School for Girls in 1887/88. Boys as well as girls were admitted to this class, which was flourishing by 1884.

Girls at the Holy Trinity Convent School in North Oxford with their teacher, *c.* 1890.

Harwell Wesleyan School group, *c.* 1893.

A cheerfully informal group of children outside Salford School, March 1905.

Mystery face; an inquisitive passer-by adds a surreal dimension to this picture of Dorchester School children in April 1905.

The first boys and girls received at the Baby School, an annexe of the Dragon School for five to eight-year-olds, founded in 1905.

Lyndon House School in Wantage, 1905. The staff and pupils of a small private school in Newbury Street which was run by Miss Bayly, the elderly woman in the back row.

Children outside Headington Quarry School, March 1906. Their clothes and even their expressions reflect the poverty that afflicted many Oxfordshire communities in the early twentieth century.

New Headington School's Infant Class on their best behaviour, c. 1906.

Keeping warm; varied headgear at Marsh Baldon School on a cold March day in 1906.

Controlled curiosity at Weston on the Green School in May 1906, as children peer through the school gate and over the wall.

Noah's Ark and a goldfish bowl add character to this Wantage group, probably taken at the National School, *c.* 1908. The school's infant teachers at that time were Miss Luckett, Miss Whitnell and Miss Vickery.

A mis-spelt 'Tempel' passes unnoticed as Temple Cowley Infants' School is photographed in 1910. The Old English sheepdog, Rebecca, belonged to the Revd George Moore, the colourful vicar of Cowley.

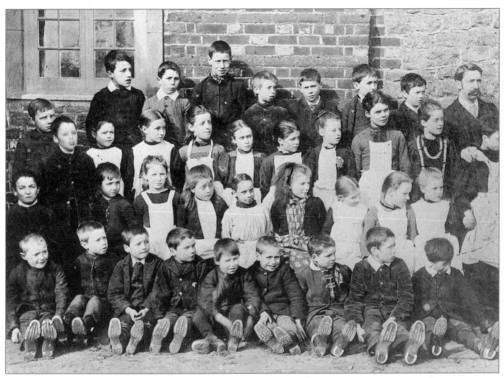

Eyes left for the children of Woodcote School, *c.* 1910. The boys in the front row are well shod for their long walks to and from school.

Empire Day group at West Hendred School, 24 May 1920. Celebrated annually from 1906, Empire Day was a time for flag-bedecked schoolrooms, patriotic songs and tableaux depicting the nation's heroes.

Teddy comes too! A little boy's favourite toy joins the children of Highmoor School, *c.* 1920.

Two boys at Oxford Wesleyan Higher Grade School in the late 1920s, identified only as R. Boasten (left) and ? Benham.

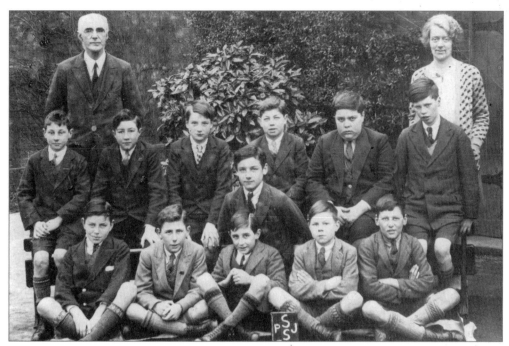

Standard V at SS Philip and James School, Oxford, 1929. Douglas Grant, who kept this photograph, is third from left in the back row; George 'Gaffer' Dent, the headmaster, and class teacher, Edith Stewart, are standing at the back.

A mixture of smiles and frowns from the children of Bladon School, photographed in the 1930s.

Proud teacher, Philip Best, at Garsington School in 1953 with his class of lower juniors.

Continuity at Ewelme in the early 1950s as teachers and pupils sit outside the fifteenth-century walls of the oldest state school in Oxfordshire, founded in 1437 by the Duke and Duchess of Suffolk.

Studied poses by Radley College boys in 1859 or 1860.

Kenneth Grahame, later famous for his book
The Wind in the Willows, was at St Edward's
School from 1869 to 1875; this photograph
was taken in about 1869.

Under the portico; young ladies of the Oxford High School for Girls in the garden of the Judge's Lodgings in St Giles' soon after the school was founded by the Girls' Public Day School Company in 1875.

A keen reader in this Magdalen College School group, *c.* 1880, raises his eyes reluctantly from his book; the Master, H.C. Ogle, prefers to be viewed in profile.

Fashionable dressers in the Shell form at Oxford High School, 1895/96.

The Lawrences at the City of Oxford High School for Boys, 1901. T.E. Lawrence, the future Lawrence of Arabia, is near the top, wearing a striped jumper; his identically dressed brothers, F.H. (front row) and W.G., are also in the group.

Self portrait; T.E. Lawrence (standing, right) took this picture himself in July 1907, using a bicycle pump under his jacket linked by rubber tubing to the camera. The school's headmaster, A.W. Cave, is seated in the centre of the group.

Douglas Bader (back row, second from left) in a group of boys from Cowell's House at St Edward's School in July 1924. Bader lost both legs in a flying accident in 1931, but went on to become an ace fighter pilot during the Second World War.

Harvest camp at Kelmscott in August 1946 with headmaster F.C. Lay at the heart of a cheerful working party from the City of Oxford High School for Boys.

Oxford High School girls, not forgetting the netball, crowd together on the school steps in 1948.

Making the best of it at Wantage Secondary Modern School, *c.* 1950. Happy students seem oblivious to the dismal Nissen hut behind them.

Prefects as they may not be remembered; smiling faces at the City of Oxford High School for Boys in 1952/53.

Through the window; the traditional way into and out of the prefects' study at Radley College in the 1950s. Visitors were seen only by invitation and many younger boys, anticipating their punishment within, must have approached this room with a heavy heart.

ACKNOWLEDGEMENTS

M ost of the photographs in this book come from the Oxfordshire Photographic Archive, a collection of over 200,000 images which is managed by Oxfordshire County Council's Department of Leisure and Arts. The Archive is based in the Centre for Oxfordshire Studies at Oxford Central Library (telephone Oxford 01865-815432) and welcomes public enquiries. Work is currently in progress to improve access to the photographs through improved documentation and the use of new technology.

The County's collections of school photographs are of special significance because of the work of Percy Elford, Oxfordshire's first Education Secretary after the Education Act of 1902. Elford photographed every Oxfordshire school inside and out while he was compiling a detailed record of all the sites which the County Council had inherited in its new role as a Local Education Authority. The resulting card index served an important administrative purpose for many years and was not formally transferred from the County Education Department to Oxfordshire Archives until 1994. In recent years, with grant aid from the Greening Lamborn Trust, the Oxfordshire Photographic Archive has commissioned conservation negatives from Elford's prints to ensure the continued existence of these historic images.

For access to other collections and much helpful advice, I am particularly indebted to the following: John Lange, Senior Museums Officer at the Vale and Downland Museum, Wantage; Ruth Escritt, archivist at the Dragon School; Brian Martin, archivist at Magdalen College School; Tony Money, archivist at Radley College, and the Bursar's secretary, Susan Brown; Elizabeth Sloan, librarian at Oxford High School for Girls; Helene van Rossum and Karen Garvey, archivists at St Edward's School; Mike Jenkins, head teacher at West Oxford School. I am also grateful to the head teachers of the following schools for permission to copy and reproduce photographs in their care: Dragon School, 41 (top), 54 (both), 62 (bottom), 75 (both), 79 (bottom), 110 (top), 113 (top); Magdalen College School, 59 (both), 71 (both), 72 (bottom), 80, 122 (bottom); Oxford High School for Girls, 17 (bottom), 21, 23 (top), 32, 37 (bottom), 40 (top), 58 (bottom), 60 (top), 61 (top), 64 (bottom), 67 (top), 87 (both), 89 (bottom), 99 (bottom), 101, 107 (bottom), 110 (bottom), 122 (top), 123 (top), 125 (bottom); Radley College, 39, 53, 56 (top), 70, 73 (top), 88 (top), 121 (top), 127; St Edward's School, 24 (top), 56 (bottom), 72 (top), 94 (bottom), 95 (top), 121 (bottom), 124 (bottom); West Oxford School, 35 (bottom), 44 (top), 50 (bottom), 90 (bottom), 93 (top).